50 Granny's Secret Recipes

By: Kelly Johnson

Table of Contents

- Granny's Classic Apple Pie
- Secret Family Meatloaf
- Old-Fashioned Chicken Pot Pie
- Granny's Homemade Biscuits
- Grandma's Slow-Cooked Beef Stew
- Secret Recipe for Buttermilk Pancakes
- Granny's Famous Chocolate Chip Cookies
- Old-School Cornbread
- Grandma's Homemade Jam
- Granny's Sunday Roast Chicken
- Secret Recipe for Creamy Mashed Potatoes
- Granny's Classic Beef Stroganoff
- Grandma's Homemade Pickles
- Secret Recipe for Tangy BBQ Sauce
- Granny's Vegetable Soup
- Classic Southern Fried Chicken
- Granny's Secret Meatball Sauce

- Old-Fashioned Peach Cobbler
- Grandma's Homemade Apple Butter
- Granny's Secret Deviled Eggs
- Classic Macaroni and Cheese
- Granny's Secret Chili Recipe
- Grandma's Buttery Dinner Rolls
- Secret Recipe for Lemon Meringue Pie
- Granny's Sweet Potato Casserole
- Classic Chicken and Dumplings
- Granny's Secret Apple Crisp
- Grandma's Homemade Sauerkraut
- Secret Recipe for Baked Ziti
- Granny's Classic Potato Salad
- Old-Fashioned Beef and Noodles
- Granny's Secret Pumpkin Pie
- Grandma's Homemade Gingerbread
- Secret Recipe for Clam Chowder
- Granny's Classic Coleslaw
- Grandma's Secret Macaroni Salad

- Old-Fashioned Banana Bread
- Granny's Secret Tomato Soup
- Classic Chicken and Rice Casserole
- Granny's Secret Blackberry Cobbler
- Grandma's Homemade Granola
- Secret Recipe for Meat Pies
- Granny's Classic Vegetable Stir Fry
- Old-Fashioned Rice Pudding
- Granny's Secret Tuna Casserole
- Grandma's Homemade Salsa
- Secret Recipe for Baked Beans
- Granny's Classic Peach Preserves
- Grandma's Secret Spaghetti Sauce
- Granny's Old-Fashioned Bread Pudding

Granny's Classic Apple Pie

Ingredients:

- 6 cups thinly sliced apples (Granny Smith or tart apples)
- 3/4 cup sugar
- 2 tbsp all-purpose flour
- 1 tsp ground cinnamon
- 1/4 tsp ground nutmeg
- 1 tbsp lemon juice
- 2 pie crusts (store-bought or homemade)

Instructions:

1. Preheat oven to 425°F (220°C).
2. Toss apples with sugar, flour, cinnamon, nutmeg, and lemon juice.
3. Line pie dish with one crust; fill with apple mixture.
4. Cover with top crust, seal edges, and cut slits for steam.
5. Bake 40-45 minutes until crust is golden and filling bubbly.

Secret Family Meatloaf

Ingredients:

- 1 1/2 lbs ground beef
- 1/2 cup breadcrumbs
- 1/2 cup milk
- 1 small onion, finely chopped
- 1 egg
- 2 tbsp ketchup
- 1 tsp Worcestershire sauce
- Salt and pepper to taste

Instructions:

1. Preheat oven to 350°F (175°C).
2. Soak breadcrumbs in milk.
3. Mix all ingredients together; shape into loaf.
4. Place in baking dish, spread ketchup on top.
5. Bake 1 hour; let rest before slicing.

Old-Fashioned Chicken Pot Pie

Ingredients:

- 2 cups cooked chicken, shredded
- 1 cup frozen mixed vegetables
- 1/3 cup butter
- 1/3 cup all-purpose flour
- 1/2 tsp salt
- 1/4 tsp pepper
- 1 3/4 cups chicken broth
- 2/3 cup milk
- 2 pie crusts

Instructions:

1. Preheat oven to 425°F (220°C).
2. In saucepan, melt butter, stir in flour, salt, and pepper until bubbly.
3. Gradually whisk in broth and milk; cook until thickened.
4. Stir in chicken and vegetables.
5. Pour into pie crust-lined dish; cover with top crust, seal edges.
6. Bake 30-35 minutes until golden.

Granny's Homemade Biscuits

Ingredients:

- 2 cups all-purpose flour
- 1 tbsp baking powder
- 1/2 tsp salt
- 1/2 cup cold butter, cubed
- 3/4 cup milk

Instructions:

1. Preheat oven to 450°F (230°C).
2. Mix flour, baking powder, and salt.
3. Cut in butter until crumbly.
4. Stir in milk until just combined.
5. Roll out and cut into rounds.
6. Bake 10-12 minutes until golden.

Grandma's Slow-Cooked Beef Stew

Ingredients:

- 2 lbs beef chuck, cubed
- 4 cups beef broth
- 3 carrots, chopped
- 3 potatoes, cubed
- 1 onion, chopped
- 2 cloves garlic, minced
- 2 tbsp tomato paste
- 2 tbsp flour
- Salt, pepper, and thyme

Instructions:

1. Brown beef in skillet; transfer to slow cooker.
2. Add vegetables, broth, garlic, tomato paste, flour, and seasonings.
3. Cook on low 7-8 hours or high 4 hours until beef is tender.

Secret Recipe for Buttermilk Pancakes

Ingredients:

- 2 cups all-purpose flour
- 2 tbsp sugar
- 2 tsp baking powder
- 1 tsp baking soda
- 1/2 tsp salt
- 2 cups buttermilk
- 2 eggs
- 1/4 cup melted butter

Instructions:

1. Whisk dry ingredients.
2. Mix buttermilk, eggs, and butter separately.
3. Combine wet and dry; stir until just combined.
4. Cook on greased griddle until bubbles form; flip and cook until golden.

Granny's Famous Chocolate Chip Cookies

Ingredients:

- 2 1/4 cups all-purpose flour
- 1 tsp baking soda
- 1/2 tsp salt
- 1 cup butter, softened
- 3/4 cup sugar
- 3/4 cup brown sugar
- 1 tsp vanilla extract
- 2 eggs
- 2 cups chocolate chips

Instructions:

1. Preheat oven to 375°F (190°C).
2. Mix flour, baking soda, and salt.
3. Cream butter and sugars; add eggs and vanilla.
4. Gradually add flour mixture.
5. Stir in chocolate chips.
6. Drop by spoonfuls onto baking sheet; bake 9-11 minutes.

Old-School Cornbread

Ingredients:

- 1 cup cornmeal
- 1 cup all-purpose flour
- 1/4 cup sugar
- 1 tbsp baking powder
- 1/2 tsp salt
- 1 cup milk
- 1/4 cup vegetable oil
- 1 egg

Instructions:

1. Preheat oven to 400°F (200°C).
2. Mix dry ingredients.
3. Whisk milk, oil, and egg.
4. Combine wet and dry.
5. Pour into greased baking pan.
6. Bake 20-25 minutes until golden.

Grandma's Homemade Jam

Ingredients:

- 4 cups fresh fruit (strawberries, raspberries, or peaches)
- 4 cups sugar
- 1/4 cup lemon juice

Instructions:

1. Crush fruit in large pot.
2. Stir in sugar and lemon juice; let sit 10 minutes.
3. Bring to boil, stirring frequently.
4. Boil hard for 1 minute, then remove from heat.
5. Pour into sterilized jars and seal.

Granny's Sunday Roast Chicken

Ingredients:

- 1 whole chicken (about 4 lbs)
- 2 tbsp olive oil
- 1 lemon, halved
- 4 garlic cloves
- Salt, pepper, and herbs (thyme, rosemary)

Instructions:

1. Preheat oven to 375°F (190°C).
2. Rub chicken with oil, season inside and out.
3. Stuff cavity with lemon and garlic.
4. Roast 1 ½ hours or until juices run clear.
5. Let rest before carving.

Secret Recipe for Creamy Mashed Potatoes

Ingredients:

- 4 large potatoes, peeled and chopped
- 1/2 cup milk
- 1/4 cup butter
- Salt and pepper

Instructions:

1. Boil potatoes until tender, drain.
2. Mash potatoes with butter and milk.
3. Season with salt and pepper to taste.
4. Serve warm and creamy.

Granny's Classic Beef Stroganoff

Ingredients:

- 1 lb beef sirloin, sliced thin
- 1 onion, chopped
- 2 cups mushrooms, sliced
- 1 cup beef broth
- 1 cup sour cream
- 2 tbsp flour
- 2 tbsp butter
- Salt and pepper

Instructions:

1. Brown beef in butter; remove and set aside.
2. Sauté onion and mushrooms until soft.
3. Sprinkle flour; stir well.
4. Add broth, cook until thickened.
5. Return beef to pan; stir in sour cream.
6. Heat through but do not boil. Serve over noodles or rice.

Grandma's Homemade Pickles

Ingredients:

- 4 cups cucumbers, sliced
- 1 cup vinegar
- 1 cup water
- 2 tbsp salt
- 2 tbsp sugar
- 2 cloves garlic
- Dill sprigs

Instructions:

1. Combine vinegar, water, salt, and sugar in pot; bring to boil.
2. Pack cucumbers, garlic, and dill into jars.
3. Pour hot brine over cucumbers; seal jars.
4. Refrigerate at least 48 hours before eating.

Secret Recipe for Tangy BBQ Sauce

Ingredients:

- 1 cup ketchup
- 1/4 cup apple cider vinegar
- 1/4 cup brown sugar
- 1 tbsp Worcestershire sauce
- 1 tsp smoked paprika
- 1/2 tsp garlic powder
- Salt and pepper

Instructions:

1. Mix all ingredients in saucepan.
2. Simmer for 15-20 minutes, stirring occasionally.
3. Cool before using as a glaze or dip.

Granny's Vegetable Soup

Ingredients:

- 2 tbsp olive oil
- 1 onion, chopped
- 2 carrots, chopped
- 2 celery stalks, chopped
- 3 cups vegetable broth
- 1 cup diced tomatoes
- 1 cup green beans, chopped
- 1 cup corn kernels
- Salt, pepper, and herbs

Instructions:

1. Heat oil; sauté onion, carrots, and celery until soft.
2. Add broth, tomatoes, and vegetables.
3. Simmer 30 minutes.
4. Season and serve hot.

Classic Southern Fried Chicken

Ingredients:

- 8 pieces chicken (legs, thighs, breasts)
- 2 cups buttermilk
- 2 cups flour
- 1 tsp paprika
- 1 tsp garlic powder
- Salt and pepper
- Oil for frying

Instructions:

1. Marinate chicken in buttermilk at least 4 hours.
2. Mix flour with spices.
3. Dredge chicken in flour mixture, shake off excess.
4. Fry in hot oil (350°F /175°C) until golden and cooked through, about 15 minutes.

Granny's Secret Meatball Sauce

Ingredients:

- 2 cups crushed tomatoes
- 1 small onion, finely chopped
- 2 cloves garlic, minced
- 1 tbsp olive oil
- 1 tsp sugar
- 1 tsp dried oregano
- Salt and pepper

Instructions:

1. Heat olive oil; sauté onion and garlic until soft.
2. Add crushed tomatoes, sugar, oregano, salt, and pepper.
3. Simmer sauce for 20-30 minutes, stirring occasionally.
4. Serve over meatballs.

Old-Fashioned Peach Cobbler

Ingredients:

- 5 cups sliced peaches
- 1 cup sugar, divided
- 1/2 cup butter, melted
- 1 cup all-purpose flour
- 1 tbsp baking powder
- 1 cup milk

Instructions:

1. Preheat oven to 375°F (190°C).
2. Toss peaches with 1/2 cup sugar; set aside.
3. Mix flour, baking powder, remaining sugar, and milk to make batter.
4. Pour melted butter into baking dish; pour batter over it (do not stir).
5. Spoon peaches on top.
6. Bake 40-45 minutes until golden and bubbly.

Grandma's Homemade Apple Butter

Ingredients:

- 4 lbs apples, peeled and sliced
- 2 cups sugar
- 1 tsp cinnamon
- 1/2 tsp cloves
- 1/2 tsp allspice

Instructions:

1. Cook apples in slow cooker on low for 10 hours, stirring occasionally.
2. Stir in sugar and spices; cook 1 more hour until thickened.
3. Blend until smooth.
4. Store in sterilized jars.

Granny's Secret Deviled Eggs

Ingredients:

- 6 hard-boiled eggs
- 3 tbsp mayonnaise
- 1 tsp Dijon mustard
- 1 tsp white vinegar
- Salt and pepper
- Paprika for garnish

Instructions:

1. Peel and halve eggs; remove yolks.
2. Mash yolks with mayonnaise, mustard, vinegar, salt, and pepper.
3. Spoon or pipe mixture back into egg whites.
4. Sprinkle with paprika.

Classic Macaroni and Cheese

Ingredients:

- 8 oz elbow macaroni
- 2 cups shredded cheddar cheese
- 2 cups milk
- 2 tbsp butter
- 2 tbsp flour
- Salt and pepper

Instructions:

1. Cook macaroni; drain.
2. Melt butter; stir in flour and cook 1 minute.
3. Gradually whisk in milk; cook until thickened.
4. Add cheese, stir until melted.
5. Mix in macaroni; season and serve.

Granny's Secret Chili Recipe

Ingredients:

- 1 lb ground beef
- 1 onion, chopped
- 1 can kidney beans, drained
- 1 can diced tomatoes
- 2 tbsp chili powder
- 1 tsp cumin
- Salt and pepper

Instructions:

1. Brown beef and onion in pot.
2. Add beans, tomatoes, and spices.
3. Simmer 30 minutes, stirring occasionally.

Grandma's Buttery Dinner Rolls

Ingredients:

- 4 cups all-purpose flour
- 1/4 cup sugar
- 1 tbsp yeast
- 1 cup warm milk
- 1/4 cup butter, melted
- 1 tsp salt
- 1 egg

Instructions:

1. Dissolve yeast in warm milk.
2. Mix flour, sugar, and salt.
3. Add milk mixture, butter, and egg; knead dough.
4. Let rise 1 hour.
5. Shape rolls; let rise 30 minutes.
6. Bake 375°F (190°C) for 15-20 minutes.

Secret Recipe for Lemon Meringue Pie

Ingredients:

- 1 prepared pie crust
- 1 1/2 cups sugar, divided
- 1/3 cup cornstarch
- 1 1/2 cups water
- 3 egg yolks, beaten
- 1/2 cup lemon juice
- 2 tbsp butter
- 3 egg whites
- 1/4 tsp cream of tartar

Instructions:

1. Prebake pie crust as directed.
2. Mix 1 1/4 cups sugar and cornstarch in saucepan; add water.
3. Cook until thickened, stirring constantly.
4. Temper egg yolks; stir into mixture.
5. Remove from heat; stir in lemon juice and butter.
6. Pour filling into crust.
7. Beat egg whites with cream of tartar until soft peaks; gradually add remaining sugar until stiff peaks.

8. Spread meringue over filling, sealing edges.

9. Bake 350°F (175°C) for 10-15 minutes until golden.

Granny's Sweet Potato Casserole

Ingredients:

- 4 cups mashed sweet potatoes
- 1/2 cup sugar
- 2 eggs, beaten
- 1/2 cup milk
- 1/2 tsp vanilla extract
- 1/2 cup butter, melted
- 1 cup brown sugar
- 1/2 cup chopped pecans
- 1/3 cup all-purpose flour
- 1/3 cup butter (for topping)

Instructions:

1. Preheat oven to 350°F (175°C).
2. Mix mashed sweet potatoes, sugar, eggs, milk, vanilla, and melted butter.
3. Pour into baking dish.
4. Combine brown sugar, pecans, flour, and butter; sprinkle on top.
5. Bake 30-35 minutes until topping is golden.

Classic Chicken and Dumplings

Ingredients:

- 1 whole chicken or 4 chicken breasts
- 6 cups chicken broth
- 3 carrots, sliced
- 2 celery stalks, sliced
- 1 onion, chopped
- 2 cups all-purpose flour
- 1 tbsp baking powder
- 1 tsp salt
- 3/4 cup milk
- 2 tbsp butter

Instructions:

1. Cook chicken in broth with vegetables until tender; remove chicken and shred.
2. Mix flour, baking powder, salt, milk, and butter to form dough.
3. Drop spoonfuls of dough into simmering broth; cook 15 minutes until dumplings are cooked through.
4. Return chicken to pot; heat through.

Granny's Secret Apple Crisp

Ingredients:

- 6 cups sliced apples
- 3/4 cup sugar
- 1 tsp cinnamon
- 1/2 cup oats
- 1/2 cup brown sugar
- 1/3 cup flour
- 1/3 cup butter, softened

Instructions:

1. Preheat oven to 350°F (175°C).
2. Toss apples with sugar and cinnamon; place in baking dish.
3. Mix oats, brown sugar, flour, and butter until crumbly.
4. Sprinkle topping over apples.
5. Bake 35-40 minutes until golden and bubbly.

Grandma's Homemade Sauerkraut

Ingredients:

- 1 medium head cabbage, shredded
- 1 tbsp salt

Instructions:

1. Toss cabbage with salt; pack tightly into clean jar.
2. Place a weight on top to keep cabbage submerged in liquid.
3. Cover jar with cloth; let ferment at room temperature 1-3 weeks, tasting regularly.
4. Refrigerate when ready.

Secret Recipe for Baked Ziti

Ingredients:

- 1 lb ziti pasta
- 2 cups marinara sauce
- 1 1/2 cups ricotta cheese
- 2 cups shredded mozzarella
- 1/2 cup grated Parmesan
- 1 egg
- Salt and pepper

Instructions:

1. Preheat oven to 375°F (190°C).
2. Cook pasta; drain.
3. Mix ricotta, egg, salt, and pepper.
4. Combine pasta, marinara, and ricotta mixture.
5. Layer pasta mixture and mozzarella in baking dish; top with Parmesan.
6. Bake 25-30 minutes until bubbly.

Granny's Classic Potato Salad

Ingredients:

- 3 lbs potatoes, peeled and cubed
- 1 cup mayonnaise
- 2 tbsp mustard
- 3 celery stalks, chopped
- 1 small onion, chopped
- Salt, pepper, and paprika

Instructions:

1. Boil potatoes until tender; drain and cool.
2. Mix mayonnaise, mustard, celery, and onion.
3. Fold in potatoes; season with salt and pepper.
4. Chill before serving; sprinkle paprika on top.

Old-Fashioned Beef and Noodles

Ingredients:

- 1 lb beef stew meat
- 4 cups beef broth
- 2 cups egg noodles
- 1 onion, chopped
- 2 tbsp flour
- Salt and pepper

Instructions:

1. Brown beef and onion in a pot.
2. Sprinkle flour and stir.
3. Add broth; simmer 1 hour until beef tender.
4. Add noodles; cook until tender.
5. Season and serve.

Granny's Secret Pumpkin Pie

Ingredients:

- 1 (15 oz) can pumpkin puree
- 3/4 cup sugar
- 1 tsp cinnamon
- 1/2 tsp ginger
- 1/4 tsp cloves
- 2 eggs
- 1 (12 oz) can evaporated milk
- 1 pie crust

Instructions:

1. Preheat oven to 425°F (220°C).
2. Mix pumpkin, sugar, and spices.
3. Beat in eggs, then stir in evaporated milk.
4. Pour into crust.
5. Bake 15 minutes; reduce heat to 350°F (175°C) and bake 40-50 minutes until set.

Grandma's Homemade Gingerbread

Ingredients:

- 2 1/4 cups all-purpose flour
- 1 tsp baking soda
- 2 tsp ground ginger
- 1 tsp cinnamon
- 1/2 tsp cloves
- 1/4 tsp nutmeg
- 1/4 tsp salt
- 1/2 cup butter, softened
- 1/2 cup brown sugar
- 1 large egg
- 3/4 cup molasses
- 3/4 cup hot water

Instructions:

1. Preheat oven to 350°F (175°C).
2. Mix flour, baking soda, and spices.
3. In a separate bowl, cream butter and sugar; beat in egg and molasses.
4. Gradually add dry ingredients alternated with hot water.

5. Pour into greased pan and bake 35-40 minutes.

Secret Recipe for Clam Chowder

Ingredients:

- 4 slices bacon, chopped
- 1 onion, chopped
- 2 celery stalks, chopped
- 2 cups potatoes, diced
- 2 cups clam juice
- 1 cup milk
- 1 cup heavy cream
- 2 cans chopped clams, drained
- Salt, pepper, and thyme

Instructions:

1. Cook bacon until crisp; remove and set aside.
2. Sauté onion and celery in bacon fat.
3. Add potatoes, clam juice, and thyme; simmer until potatoes are tender.
4. Stir in clams, milk, and cream; heat through without boiling.
5. Season and garnish with bacon.

Granny's Classic Coleslaw

Ingredients:

- 1 small head cabbage, shredded
- 2 carrots, grated
- 1/2 cup mayonnaise
- 2 tbsp apple cider vinegar
- 1 tbsp sugar
- Salt and pepper

Instructions:

1. Toss cabbage and carrots.
2. Mix mayonnaise, vinegar, sugar, salt, and pepper.
3. Combine dressing with vegetables.
4. Chill before serving.

Grandma's Secret Macaroni Salad

Ingredients:

- 2 cups cooked elbow macaroni
- 1/2 cup mayonnaise
- 1/4 cup sour cream
- 1/2 cup diced celery
- 1/4 cup chopped onion
- 1 tbsp pickle relish
- Salt and pepper

Instructions:

1. Mix mayonnaise and sour cream.
2. Add celery, onion, relish, salt, and pepper.
3. Stir in cooked macaroni.
4. Refrigerate before serving.

Old-Fashioned Banana Bread

Ingredients:

- 3 ripe bananas, mashed
- 1/3 cup melted butter
- 3/4 cup sugar
- 1 egg, beaten
- 1 tsp vanilla extract
- 1 tsp baking soda
- Pinch of salt
- 1 1/2 cups all-purpose flour

Instructions:

1. Preheat oven to 350°F (175°C).
2. Mix mashed bananas and butter.
3. Stir in sugar, egg, and vanilla.
4. Sprinkle baking soda and salt over mixture.
5. Add flour and mix.
6. Pour into greased loaf pan; bake 60 minutes.

Granny's Secret Tomato Soup

Ingredients:

- 2 tbsp butter
- 1 onion, chopped
- 2 cans (14 oz) crushed tomatoes
- 2 cups chicken broth
- 1 tsp sugar
- Salt and pepper
- 1/2 cup cream

Instructions:

1. Melt butter; sauté onion until soft.
2. Add tomatoes, broth, sugar, salt, and pepper.
3. Simmer 20 minutes.
4. Blend until smooth.
5. Stir in cream; heat through.

Classic Chicken and Rice Casserole

Ingredients:

- 2 cups cooked chicken, shredded
- 1 cup uncooked rice
- 2 cups chicken broth
- 1 can cream of mushroom soup
- 1 cup shredded cheddar cheese
- Salt and pepper

Instructions:

1. Preheat oven to 350°F (175°C).
2. Mix chicken, rice, broth, soup, salt, and pepper in baking dish.
3. Cover and bake 45 minutes.
4. Top with cheese; bake 10 minutes until melted.

Granny's Secret Blackberry Cobbler

Ingredients:

- 4 cups fresh blackberries
- 1 cup sugar, divided
- 1 cup all-purpose flour
- 1 tsp baking powder
- 1/2 tsp salt
- 1 cup milk
- 1/2 cup butter, melted

Instructions:

1. Preheat oven to 375°F (190°C).
2. Toss blackberries with 1/2 cup sugar; place in baking dish.
3. Mix flour, baking powder, salt, remaining sugar, and milk to make batter.
4. Pour melted butter into baking dish; pour batter over butter (do not stir).
5. Spoon blackberries on top.
6. Bake 40-45 minutes until golden.

Grandma's Homemade Granola

Ingredients:

- 3 cups rolled oats
- 1 cup chopped nuts (almonds, walnuts, etc.)
- 1/2 cup shredded coconut (optional)
- 1/3 cup honey or maple syrup
- 1/4 cup vegetable oil
- 1 tsp vanilla extract
- 1/2 tsp cinnamon
- 1 cup dried fruit (raisins, cranberries, etc.)

Instructions:

1. Preheat oven to 300°F (150°C).
2. Mix oats, nuts, coconut, and cinnamon in a bowl.
3. In a separate bowl, whisk honey, oil, and vanilla.
4. Combine wet and dry ingredients; spread on baking sheet.
5. Bake 25-30 minutes, stirring halfway, until golden.
6. Cool, then stir in dried fruit.

Secret Recipe for Meat Pies

Ingredients:

- 1 lb ground beef or lamb
- 1 onion, chopped
- 1/2 cup peas and carrots (optional)
- 1/2 cup beef broth
- 1 tbsp Worcestershire sauce
- Salt and pepper
- Pie crust dough (store-bought or homemade)

Instructions:

1. Brown meat and onion in a skillet.
2. Add peas, carrots, broth, Worcestershire sauce; simmer until thickened.
3. Season with salt and pepper; cool filling.
4. Roll out dough; cut into circles or squares.
5. Place filling in dough, fold, and seal edges.
6. Bake at 375°F (190°C) for 25-30 minutes until golden.

Granny's Classic Vegetable Stir Fry

Ingredients:

- 2 cups mixed vegetables (broccoli, bell peppers, carrots, snap peas)
- 2 tbsp vegetable oil
- 2 cloves garlic, minced
- 1 tbsp soy sauce
- 1 tsp sesame oil
- Salt and pepper

Instructions:

1. Heat oil in wok or skillet.
2. Stir-fry garlic until fragrant.
3. Add vegetables; cook until crisp-tender.
4. Stir in soy sauce and sesame oil; season with salt and pepper.
5. Serve hot.

Old-Fashioned Rice Pudding

Ingredients:

- 1 cup cooked rice
- 2 cups milk
- 1/2 cup sugar
- 1 tsp vanilla extract
- 1/2 tsp cinnamon
- 1/4 tsp salt
- 2 eggs, beaten
- 1/2 cup raisins (optional)

Instructions:

1. In a saucepan, combine cooked rice, milk, sugar, vanilla, cinnamon, and salt.
2. Cook over medium heat until thick and creamy.
3. Temper eggs by adding hot mixture slowly to beaten eggs, then stir back into saucepan.
4. Cook 2 more minutes, stirring constantly.
5. Stir in raisins.
6. Serve warm or chilled.

Granny's Secret Tuna Casserole

Ingredients:

- 2 cups cooked pasta (egg noodles preferred)
- 1 can (10.5 oz) cream of mushroom soup
- 1 cup milk
- 1 can (5 oz) tuna, drained
- 1 cup frozen peas
- 1 cup shredded cheddar cheese
- 1/2 cup breadcrumbs

Instructions:

1. Preheat oven to 350°F (175°C).
2. Mix soup and milk; stir in pasta, tuna, peas, and half the cheese.
3. Pour into baking dish; top with remaining cheese and breadcrumbs.
4. Bake 25-30 minutes until bubbly and golden.

Grandma's Homemade Salsa

Ingredients:

- 4 ripe tomatoes, diced
- 1 small onion, finely chopped
- 1 jalapeño, seeded and minced
- 2 cloves garlic, minced
- 1/4 cup fresh cilantro, chopped
- Juice of 1 lime
- Salt and pepper to taste

Instructions:

1. Combine all ingredients in a bowl.
2. Mix well and refrigerate for at least 1 hour to let flavors meld.
3. Serve chilled with chips or as a topping.

Secret Recipe for Baked Beans

Ingredients:

- 4 cups cooked navy beans (or 2 cans, drained)
- 1/2 cup brown sugar
- 1/2 cup molasses
- 1 onion, chopped
- 4 slices bacon, chopped
- 1/4 cup ketchup
- 1 tbsp mustard
- Salt and pepper to taste

Instructions:

1. Preheat oven to 350°F (175°C).
2. Cook bacon until crisp; remove and set aside.
3. In bacon fat, sauté onion until translucent.
4. Combine beans, bacon, onion, brown sugar, molasses, ketchup, and mustard in a baking dish.
5. Bake uncovered for 1 hour, stirring occasionally.

Granny's Classic Peach Preserves

Ingredients:

- 4 cups peeled, chopped peaches
- 3 cups sugar
- 2 tbsp lemon juice
- 1/2 tsp ground cinnamon (optional)

Instructions:

1. Combine peaches, sugar, and lemon juice in a large pot.
2. Cook over medium heat, stirring frequently, until mixture thickens (about 30-40 minutes).
3. Add cinnamon if desired.
4. Pour into sterilized jars and seal.

Grandma's Secret Spaghetti Sauce

Ingredients:

- 2 tbsp olive oil
- 1 onion, chopped
- 4 cloves garlic, minced
- 2 cans (28 oz each) crushed tomatoes
- 1 tbsp tomato paste
- 1 tbsp sugar
- 1 tsp dried oregano
- 1 tsp dried basil
- Salt and pepper to taste
- Fresh basil for garnish (optional)

Instructions:

1. Heat olive oil; sauté onion and garlic until soft.
2. Stir in crushed tomatoes, tomato paste, sugar, oregano, and basil.
3. Simmer uncovered for 45 minutes to an hour.
4. Season with salt and pepper.
5. Serve over cooked spaghetti and garnish with fresh basil.

Granny's Old-Fashioned Bread Pudding

Ingredients:

- 6 cups cubed day-old bread
- 4 cups milk
- 3/4 cup sugar
- 3 eggs
- 2 tsp vanilla extract
- 1 tsp cinnamon
- 1/2 cup raisins (optional)

Instructions:

1. Preheat oven to 350°F (175°C).
2. Soak bread cubes in milk for 10 minutes.
3. Whisk sugar, eggs, vanilla, and cinnamon together.
4. Combine with bread mixture; fold in raisins if desired.
5. Pour into greased baking dish.
6. Bake 45-50 minutes until set and golden.

www.ingramcontent.com/pod-product-compliance
Lightning Source LLC
LaVergne TN
LVHW081322060526
838201LV00055B/2407